Judy Horacek is a freelance cartoonist, illustrator and writer. Her work has appeared in *The Age*, *The Australian* and *The Canberra Times*, and a multitude of other publications. Her strong sassy female characters can be found on fridges and toilet doors all over the world. She is currently published regularly in *The Age*. Major retrospective exhibitions of her cartoons have been held at the National Museum of Australia and the National Gallery of Victoria. She has twice been nominated for Walkley Awards. Judy also creates children's picture books – both on her own and in collaboration with Mem Fox. Together Mem and Judy created the bestselling *Where is the Green Sheep?* which became an instant children's classic. They have now done four books together. Judy's cartoons feature in greeting card ranges in both Australia and the UK, and she also regularly exhibits her limited edition prints and watercolours. Her website is www.horacek.com.au

Random Life is her ninth published cartoon collection.

BOOKS BY JUDY HORACEK

CARTOON BOOKS

If You Can't Stand the Heat (2010)
Make Cakes Not War (2006)
I Am Woman, Hear Me Draw (first edition 2002, revised edition 2013)
If the Fruit Fits (1999)
Lost in Space (1997)
Woman with Altitude (1997)
Unrequited Love Nos. 1-100 (1994)
Life on the Edge (1992, revised edition 2003)

CHILDREN'S BOOKS

Solo
Yellow is My Colour Star (2014, first published as *Yellow is My Favourite Colour* 2010)
These are My Hands/These are My Feet (2011, first published as separate volumes:
These are My Feet 2008 and *These are My Hands* 2009)
The Story of Growl (2007)

With Mem Fox
Where is the Green Sheep? (2004)
Good Night Sleep Tight (2012)
This & That (2015)
Ducks Away! (2016)

OTHER BOOKS

With Mem Fox
Reading Magic (2001)

With Doug MacLeod
The Night Before Mother's Day (2012)

www.horacek.com.au

RANDOM LIFE

cartoons by
judy horacek

with a foreword by
john clarke

horacek
PRESS

www.horacek.com.au

To Francesca, for her love and her infinite patience
with me and my projects

Horacek Press
PO Box 231
Brunswick East, Victoria 3057, Australia
Email: info@horacek.com.au

First published by Horacek Press, 2017

Distributed by Schwartz Publishing Pty Ltd
Level 1, 221 Drummond Street
Carlton VIC 3053, Australia
enquiries@blackincbooks.com

Printed and bound in Australia by Ligare
Design by DesignEdge www.design-edge.com.au

National Library of Australia
Cataloguing-in-Publication data

Horacek, Judy, 1961-
Random Life : cartoons by Judy Horacek
ISBN: 9780987612908 (paperback)

Caricatures and cartoons.
Wit and humor, Pictorial.
741.5994

www.horacek.com.au

FOREWORD

If you're not brought up in Australia, the things that impress
you when you arrive here are the sheer space and flatness of the
place, the remarkable birds, and the quality and audacity of the
cartoonists. Like the birds, the cartoonists are beautifully adapted
to their habitat and are varied in their use of it. And like the birds,
some have powerful beaks and sharp talons, others are elegant
but are shy and seldom seen. Some squawk, some whistle,
some cry.

In this unique island landscape, Judy Horacek is a honeyeater:
agile, industrious and singing her position as she darts from
plant to plant.

Sticking with the bird analogy, Judy is rather rare. Her style is
distinctive and for many years I have sought her cartoons in
the mainstream press possibly because she is idiosyncratic and
always at a slight angle to the rest of the publication. She's not
the main editorial cartoonist and is perhaps not even quite in
the main stream of cartooning at all. She has carved out a niche
for herself, which perhaps only she and the readers understand.
In his introduction to one of Judy's earlier books, her wise

colleague Peter Nicholson suggests a reason for this in describing the internal scrutiny of cartoons before the public sees them:

> If you are working as a professional cartoonist you live in a very competitive world. Every time you submit a cartoon for publication it gets judged a number of times – once by the editor before it goes into the publication, once by the public when they see it. If you're moving into book publication, the book publisher will make a judgment, too. But first of all it is judged by the cartoonist him or herself.[*]

Judy is a very deft judge. This might be instinctive and it might be the result of careful analysis. It might just be the search for honey. Whatever it is, it works. I've been trusting Judy's judgment for twenty years and have been taken to parts of the forest I've never been before.

Cartoonists are important in Australia in a way in which their rich and powerful employers are not. They are listened to in a way in which elected representatives and other celebrity chefs are not. Of all the public figures in Australia, the group with whom the people feel a sense of intimacy is the cartoonists. This is interesting because the public doesn't really know the cartoonists; it knows the cartoons. The cartoons resonate against the thoughts and feelings and memories of readers, and the readers thereby contribute to the creative process of understanding the cartoon. This process is an enormous secret and some cartoonists are very deft at leaving enough room for it to happen.

Judy can be funny about almost anything and in this collection of work from the last six years we see the range and sharp humour of her work and we also see a consistent world view. It is a feminist view, an egalitarian and inclusive view, and it is not a view to be pushed around. It bites. It's not always clear whether your laughter and delight are comforting to your perspective on a particular issue or are giving it a swift kick in the pants. This too, is rare and helpful. And since Judy's is a creative process whose main characteristics include a sublime subjectivity and a lightness of touch, I don't wish to add further to the lead balloon of analysis. So I'll stop now.

Judy Horacek is an alternative fact of the most engaging and necessary kind. Long may she reign.

John Clarke
March 2017

* Peter Nicholson, Introduction to *If the Fruit Fits – cartoons by Judy Horacek*, Hodder Headline, 1999

INTRODUCTION

When I began cartooning, I really did believe that some well-aimed cartoons could change people's minds – that everyone would realise the commonsense of things like treating people equally, of not destroying the environment in which we live and on which we depend. And so on. Clearly this was foolish, and perhaps I shouldn't keep mentioning it. But the thing is I'm still trying – lack of success to date notwithstanding – because drawing pictures is the best weapon I have.

Maybe nowadays I do more cartoons that are simply silly and not particularly political. This isn't the creep of conservatism that affects some cartoonists, it's more because I think silly is a fantastic part of life. Talking animals, hybrid creatures, dreadful puns, rewriting fairytales – it's all very enjoyable. As is taking the mickey out of things – the contemporary obsession with coffee for example, which is a recurring theme in this book. Such cartoons are also a brilliant break from the direness of the world. I don't actually believe that if we all laughed more the world would be a better place (I might be foolish but I'm not that foolish) but it definitely wouldn't hurt.

The majority of the cartoons in this book were first published in *The Age*, Melbourne's Fairfax newspaper, where I have had a regular weekly spot since mid-2012. My first regular day there was Monday, which is one reason why there are so many cartoons in this book about that day. The other reason is, well, Monday.

Other cartoons in this collection were first published in *Overland*, the long-running progressive literary journal, which featured my cartoons from early 2011 until the end of 2013, and in *Sheilas*, a monthly online feminist journal published by the Victorian Women's Trust from July 2012 until September 2016 every issue of which featured a Horacek. I'm also often published in the *Walkley Magazine*. The cartoon on the facing page was the cover of the December 2012 edition, and I love the way it sums up so much about how life is for women in contemporary society, 'diving in *in spite of everything*' (italics added).

The two pages 'Here in the everyday' and 'Some things I know' were commissioned for *Drawn From Life: Stories from the Everyday*, a giveaway 'newspaper' edited by Oslo Davis, featuring cartoonists from Australia and round the world, a project of the 2011 Melbourne Writers Festival. It's not a literal truth of my everyday, but it does capture something of my thought processes.

It's a difficult time to be a cartoonist nowadays. The medium of cartooning is quite possibly in danger, because the places where cartoons were mostly published, newspapers and magazines, are in a bad way. This isn't to say that new and wonderful things aren't going to take their place – Exhibit A: the Internet. But the world I grew up in, that of newspapers with their own individual cartoonists reflecting on things internationally and locally is over. This make me sad. In many ways, it affects me less than it does other cartoonists, because I've only ever been part of that world tangentially. In order to make a living, I have always had to find other places to moor my cartoons as well, like greeting cards and merchandise. I've also been lucky enough to be able to make my way into the amazing world of children's picture books. And I do more 'arty' things, such as prints and watercolours that I exhibit. All this has enabled me to cobble together a patchwork kind of career, one that has brought me a lot of joy (and an extraordinary number of working hours). This book is peppered with cartoons about the work/life balance, so it's clearly something I think about a lot, with little progress. But at least it's good material for cartoons.

It's a difficult time to be a cartoonist for another reason as well. People assume that having dreadful politicians makes it easier to come up with cartoon ideas; we cartoonists get told often how lucky we are right now. But the opposite is true – the political ideas around now are so extraordinary that there is almost nothing you can do with them. One of the most powerful tools of cartoonists and comedians is exaggeration to the point of absurdity, to reveal how rotten something is. And now those kinds of words and policies are coming out of politicians' mouths for real. So many examples – arguments for tax cuts for the rich and wage cuts for the poor; talk of 'clean coal'; anti-science and anti-knowledge statements, to name just a few. People in power are currently self-satirising to an alarming extent, and it makes the job of cartoonists and other funny people much more difficult. And also makes the world much scarier.

I am nowhere more aware of this than in Australia's treatment of refugees and asylum seekers. Where once the government tried to deter refugees from coming to Australia using a campaign about dangerous things like spiders and snakes (I remember doing a cartoon about this in 2000), now the deterrence takes the form of actual human rights abuses. It is chilling to hear them speak of indefinite incarceration and disavowal of our legal obligations towards fellow human beings with the 'justification' that this is for some greater good. It's impossible to exaggerate the Orwellian double-speak; one can only listen in disbelief.

In spite of this difficulty, I still try to do cartoons about these issue, and there are a number of them in this book, mostly first published in *The Age*. Some of these have subsequently been republished elsewhere many times, particularly by refugee rights groups. I particularly want to mention the cartoon on page 230 which was drawn for a campaign to raise awareness of the plight of a young Iranian cartoonist, whose pen name is 'Eaten Fish'. He is currently in his fourth year of detention on Manus Island. The campaign was organised by First Dog on the Moon and the *Guardian Australia* and involved many cartoonists. Our cartoons haven't fixed anything, (see opening paragraph) but they have raised awareness of the issue around the world.

When we are in danger of losing our planet through environmental destruction, and losing our humanity through our treatment of other people, and we never actually got to equality of the sexes, what do we have left?

Random Life contains cartoons about very important issues, and cartoons that are totally off the wall. I've done my best to arrange them so that the experience of straight-out funny and the experience of 'you have to laugh or you'll cry', or even just 'you have to cry', don't bump up uncomfortably against each other. When it comes down to it, life taken randomly is mix of all these things.

Random Life is my ninth cartoon collection, which is a pretty significant achievement. The other books have all been with well-respected publishers, but in keeping with the DIY nature of most of my career, I decided to have a go at doing it all myself. This book is thus the first publication of the newly born Horacek Press. From my point of view, being the publisher as well as the content provider has been best of times and also the worst of times. I now present to you *Random Life*.

I hope you enjoy it.

judy horacek

Every journey begins with a single step.
Are you sure? I thought it was a double espresso.
horacek

HOW THE MUNDANE CAN RUIN YOUR FANTASIES
Wheeeee!!!
Where on earth will I park this thing?
horacek

You're a dinosaur. What're you doing in my bathroom?
Is that some sort of trick question?
horacek

The Passive-Aggressive Elephant-in-the-Room

horacek

I can't believe the madonna/whore thing is still as strong as ever
Plus now you have to be both at the same time
horacek

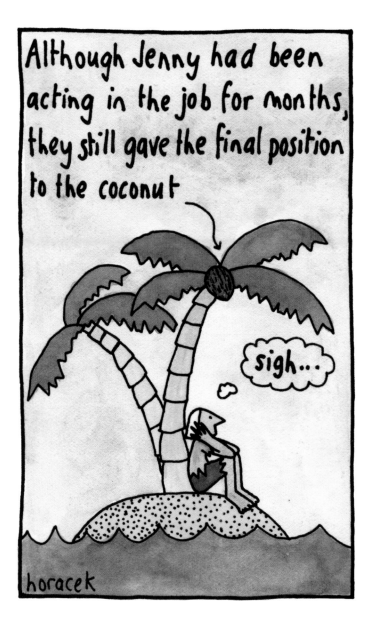

26

Susie knew that the carpet wasn't really magic, but at this point it seemed best to keep that to herself...

Seemed Like A Good Idea At The Time No. 43 'Tomato Frisbee'

horacek

Breakfast meetings were one thing - but surely beach meetings are going a step too far

I'd be happy to draw a line in the sand

horacek

THE JACK QUIZ
'HOW <u>DULL</u> ARE YOU?'

A. All play, no work

B. Some work, some play

C. All work, no play

D. Too busy worrying about work/play balance to do much of either

horacek

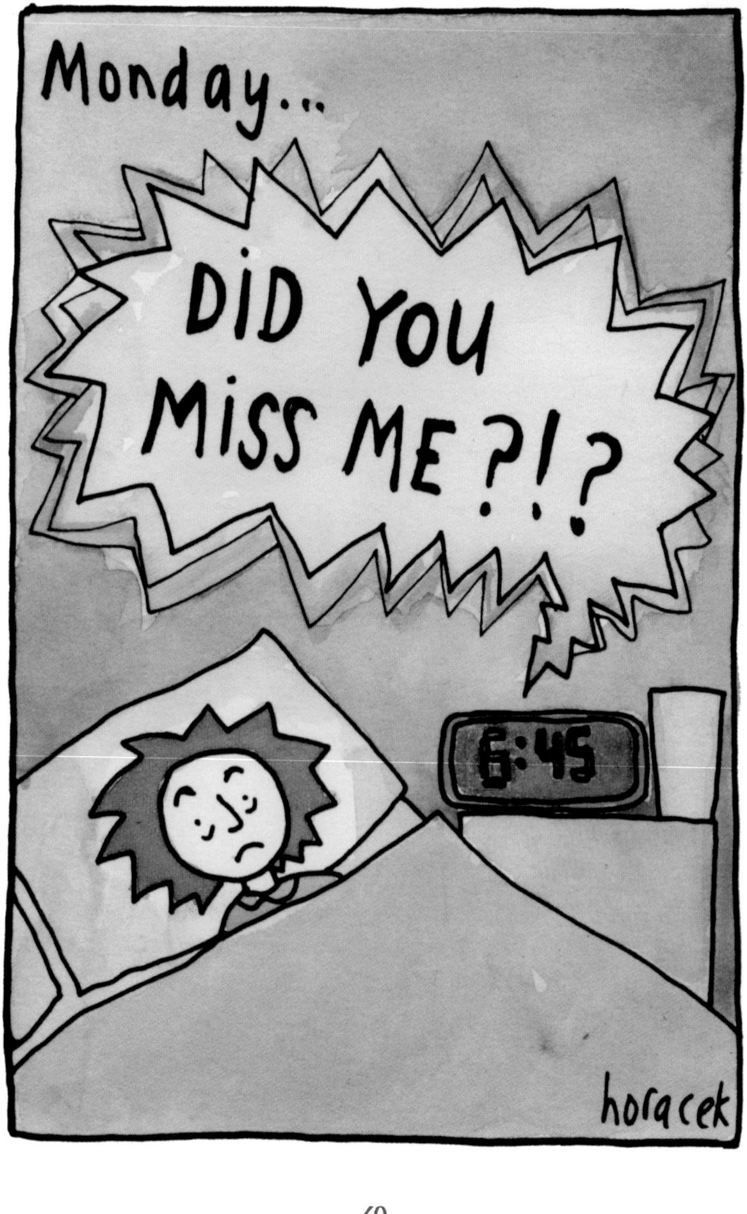
Monday...
DID YOU MISS ME?!?
6:45
horacek

Hey, our words are appearing above our heads
We must be on some sort of cartoon cam
horacek

46

48

Just how am I supposed to dream the impossible dream if I have to drink the undrinkable coffee?
horacek

50

Humpty Trumpy sat on a wall
Horacek
Humpty Trumpy had a great call
I'll make America great again!
And all the 'small hand' jokes, and all the 'orange skin' jibes, didn't stop him from winning the President prize.
Ha, ha, suckers!
Wasn't he supposed to, like, fall?
Sigh

55

Pavlov's Cats
Those dogs have no self-respect
Ding, ding, ding drool, drool, drool. Pitiful, really pitiful...
horacek

Once again the clowns had been caught kissing instead of practising.

horacek

Fairy Tales go Healthy:
Hansel and Gretel
Be careful Hansel- don't forget your portion sizing!

65

Art materials: $235·26
Tools: $356·84
A career in the arts: priceless
And for everything else, there's dumpster diving
horacek

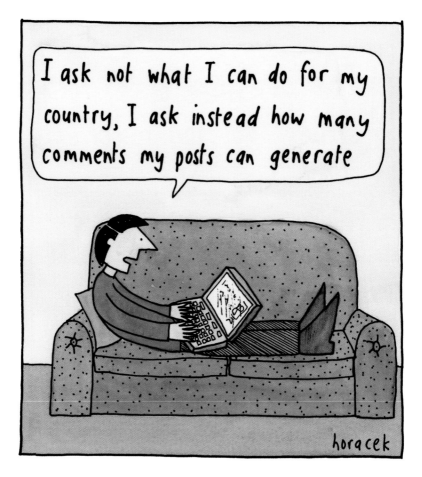

i-Dream of Jeannie

horacek

75

DAVID BOWIE'S ARACHNIDS

The world-famous Spiders from Mars

along with the less well-known

Scorpion from Saturn

and the

Ticks from Jupiter (incl. moons)

horacek

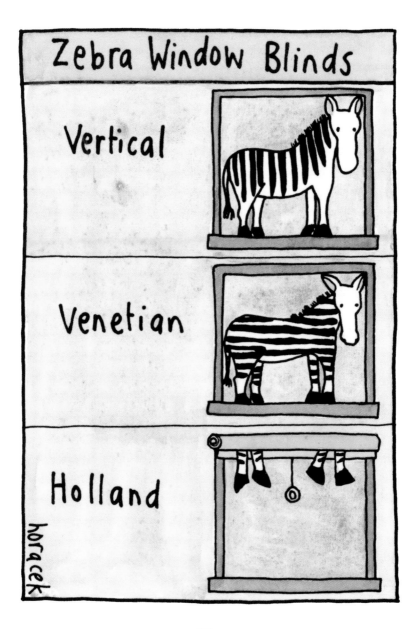

THE WORLD'S BIGGEST LOSER GRAND FINALE
Okay then, tied for second place are the rainforests & the polar ice caps - both have lost thousands of square kilometres & are still losing area at a phenomenal rate! Which means that first place in The World's Biggest Loser goes to...
The human race!!!
APPLAUSE

Skin protection I can understand, but why all this hoo-ha about protecting our boardies?
horacek

Oh no, it's those awful teapot people heading this way
What's the bet they make that storm in a teacup joke again
horacek

93

I'm tired of being called a latte-sipping leftie
You show them then - seize that latte and GULP it down!
horacek

It's always about you, isn't it?
It is not! Quite often it's about the coffee
horacek

Really? Your contact on The Other Side is a chicken?
Of course. Why else do you think it crossed the road?
horacek

Please try not to worry dear – I'm sure it won't be long before there's a Transplant App

horacek

107

108

Noughts and Crosses FOI Request

horacek

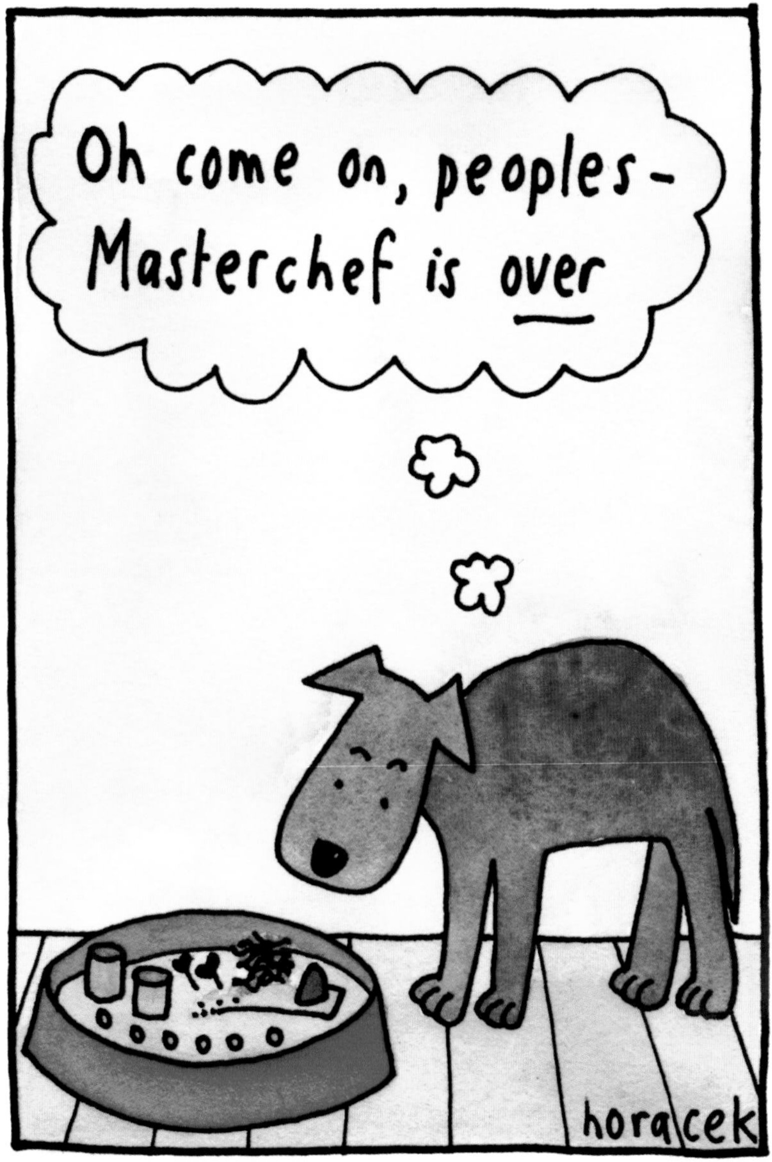
Oh come on, peoples -
Masterchef is over
horacek

119

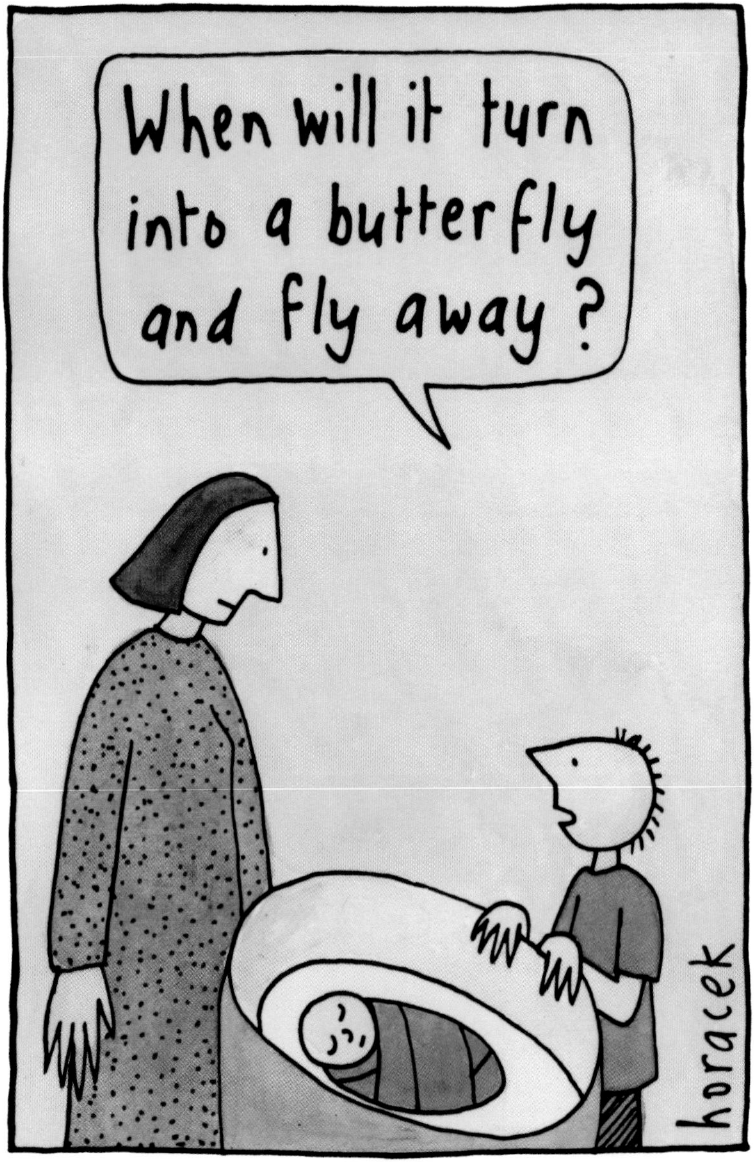
When will it turn into a butterfly and fly away?
horacek

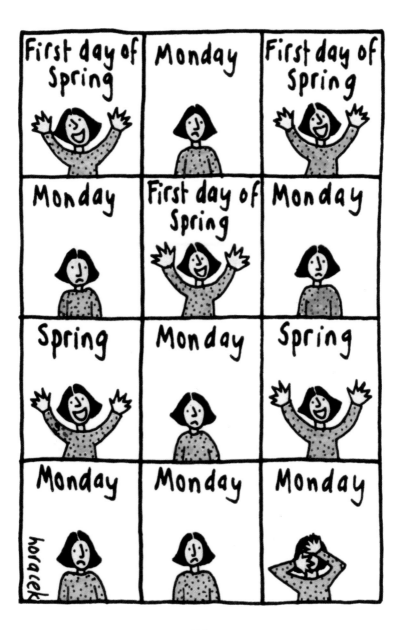

Deconstructed food is so passé -I've moved on to Unconstructed now
horacek

Psst - remind me again what we're announcing now - is it "Yeah...nah" or "Nah...yeah...nah"?
horacek

127

Modern Love
How's my love poem going?
I can't believe nothing rhymes with 'emoticon'
horacek

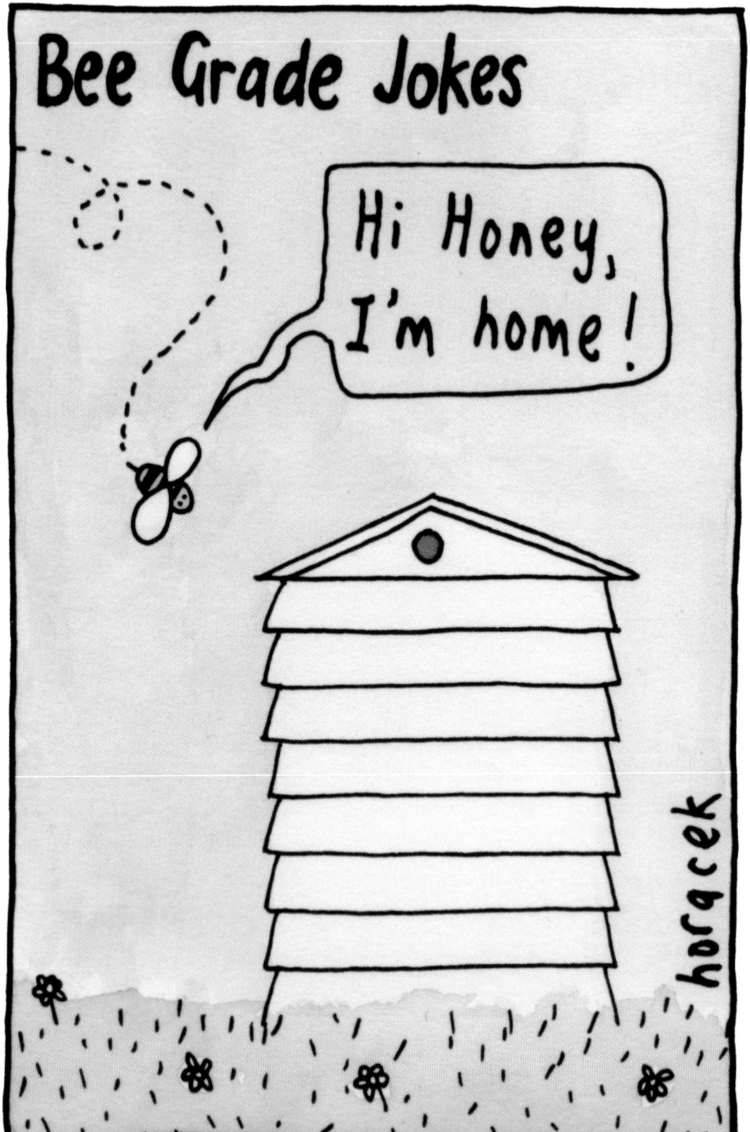
Bee Grade Jokes
Hi Honey, I'm home!
horacek

Well I was over there & I thought, why cross? Then I thought, why not? & here I am, on the other side...
Wow, that's exactly how it was for me! Do you think it's some kind of joke?
horacek

Won't you ever change?
I'm a stick in the mud, get used to it.
horacek

OLD

pissing into the wind

NEW

trying to stop renewables by blaming windpower for electricity outages

horacek

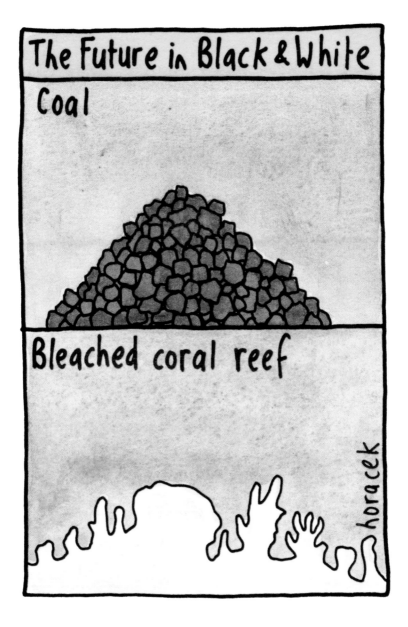

The New Sour Grapes
Bah! So what if I can't reach - they're probably sour anyway
Ha ha ha, they're plastic
horacek

A kangaroo writes a haiku, and recites it to a cockatoo.
Whoopy-do
horacek

So...what's this, umm... slime?
We're trying out the new primeval diet. Cool, huh?
horacek

The Very End of the Footy Season

That's the last two heading off to join the others

Wonder where they go?

horacek

146

Ideas in need of a slight redesign: Umbrella phones
Hello?..Oh hi Sue, hang on I'm getting really wet here
horacek

Vampires Go Vegetarian
Not blood oranges for dinner again?
horacek

If Tongues did Cross-stitch
HOME SWEET HOME
HOME SOUR HOME
HOME BITTER HOME
HOME SALTY HOME
horacek

Monday Haiku

The new week strung with
days of work, like beads to be
worn, and be worn by.

horacek

In prehistoric times, people lived in caves in the rock
That must've played hell with their wireless connections
horacek

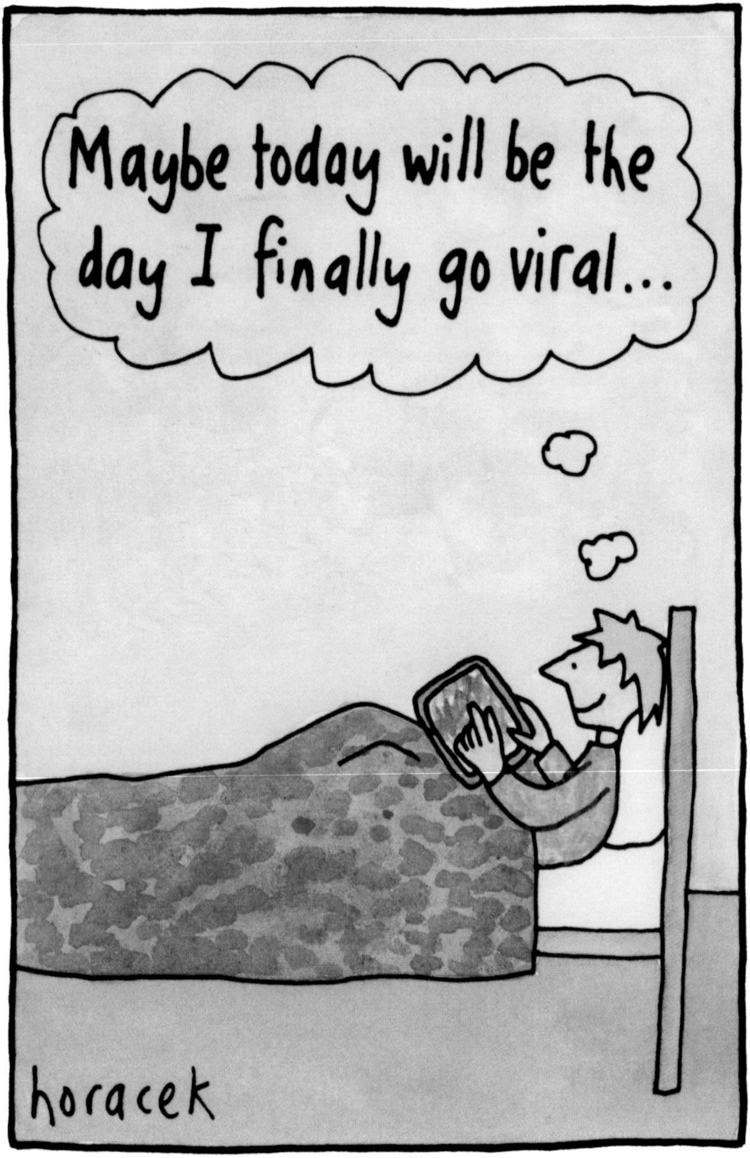
Maybe today will be the day I finally go viral...
horacek

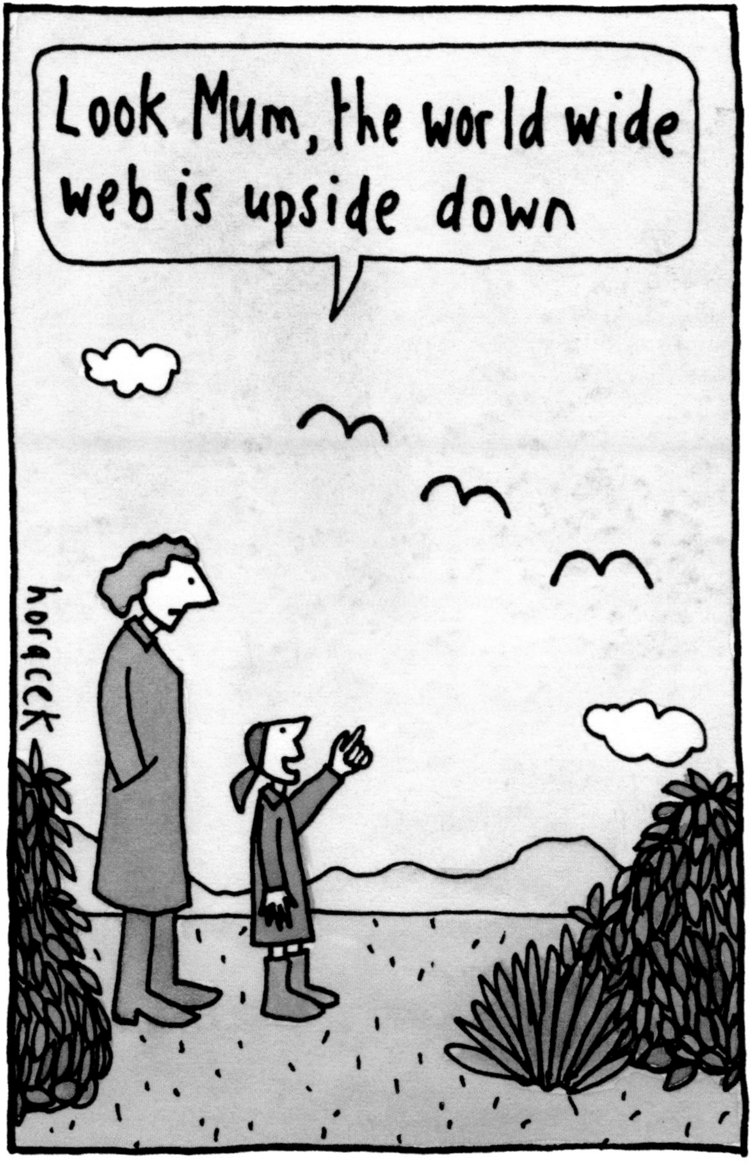
Look Mum, the world wide web is upside down
horacek

The Glass Ceiling

Don't just stand there — polish it or something.

horacek

156

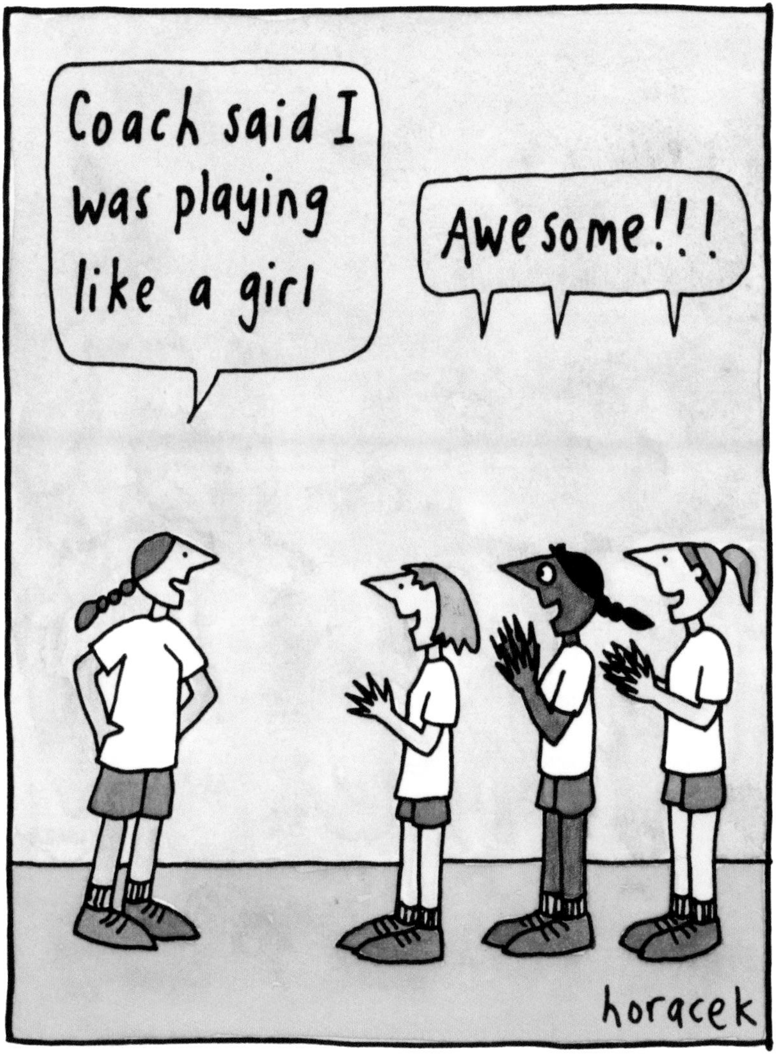
Coach said I was playing like a girl
Awesome!!!
horacek

So is it our fundamental task to get the basics right, or is it our basic task to get the fundamentals right?
What do the focus groups say?
horacek

There goes the neighbourhood

horacek

Climate change is only a theory
A theory like the theory of gravity?
What?! Gravity is a theory as well? Damn scientists with their plots and conspiracies!
Well, I'm not going to be fooled. No 'theories' for me!
Hey...
horacek

169

horacek

Star light, star bright,
looking down upon our plight,
deadly displays of
             Strength and Might —
Wish you could put the world to right.

The girls in the office say they are sick of our casual sexism
What, the cuties want us to dress up for it?
horacek

Limerick for a 21st century feminist
There once was a girl who spoke up,
She knew women's rights weren't just a matter of luck.
The trolls went on the attack,
But she keeps fighting back-
That girl who speaks up sure has pluck.
Ha! You neanderthals won't silence me!
horacek
Did you spot the error in the title? Yes - this limerick does apply to feminists of all times, present and past.

Smiley
face

Frowny
face

Electrical
plug

horacek

Don't seem out-of-date at your climate change denial rally -
CHECK OUT OUR NEW RANGE OF T's
Planet Schmanet
STOP THE SCIENCE
Every species for itself
SUCK MY EMISSIONS
horacek

187

21st century superheroes

Able to leap tall buildings in a single bound while texting

horacek

horacek

189

Winter Singlet Haiku
Singlets keep you warm,
especially all tucked in.
Mmmm. Feel the cosy.
Snug as a bug in a singlet
horacek

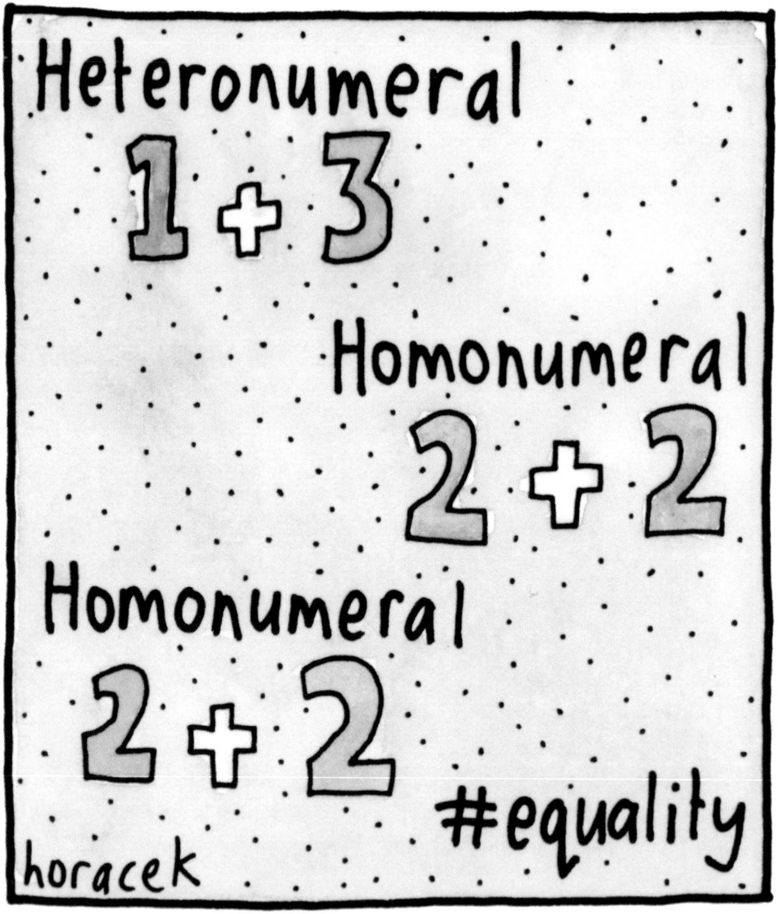
Heteronumeral
1 + 3
Homonumeral
2 + 2
Homonumeral
2 + 2
#equality
horacek

Gilligan's Parking Meter

horacek

199

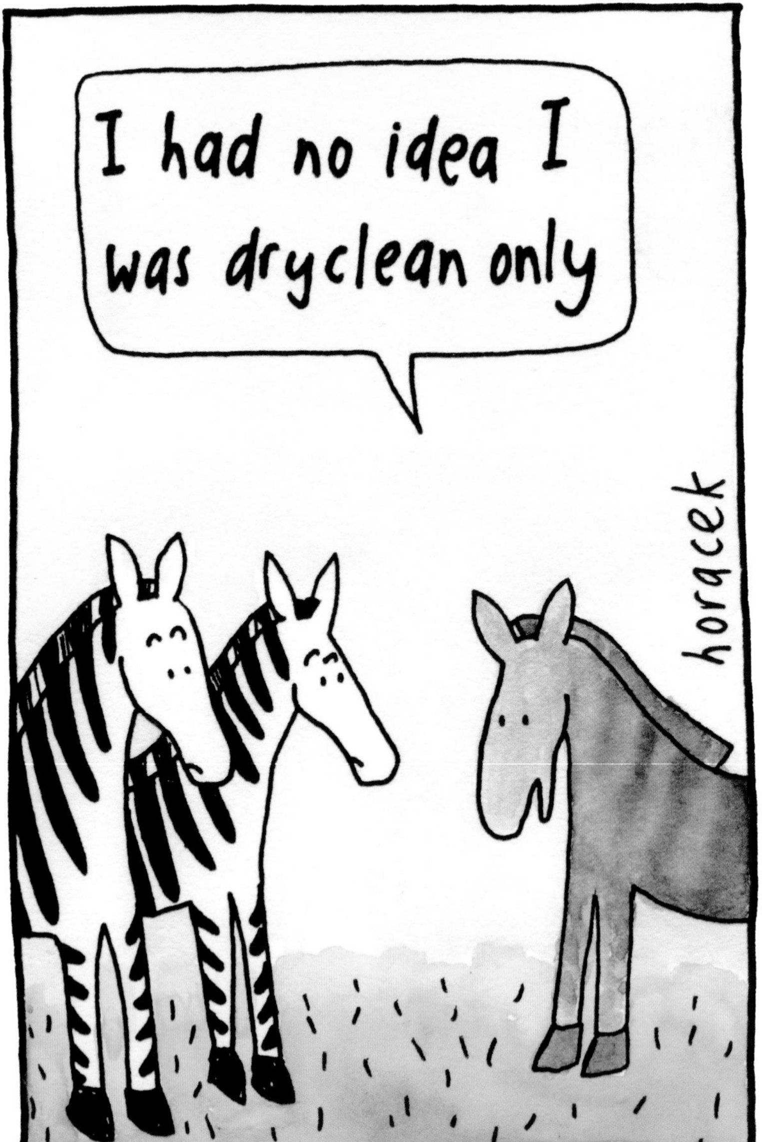
I had no idea I was dryclean only
horacek

You know very well I meant you to go outside, not to 'get some fresh air' by searching the Net
FRESH AIR
horacek

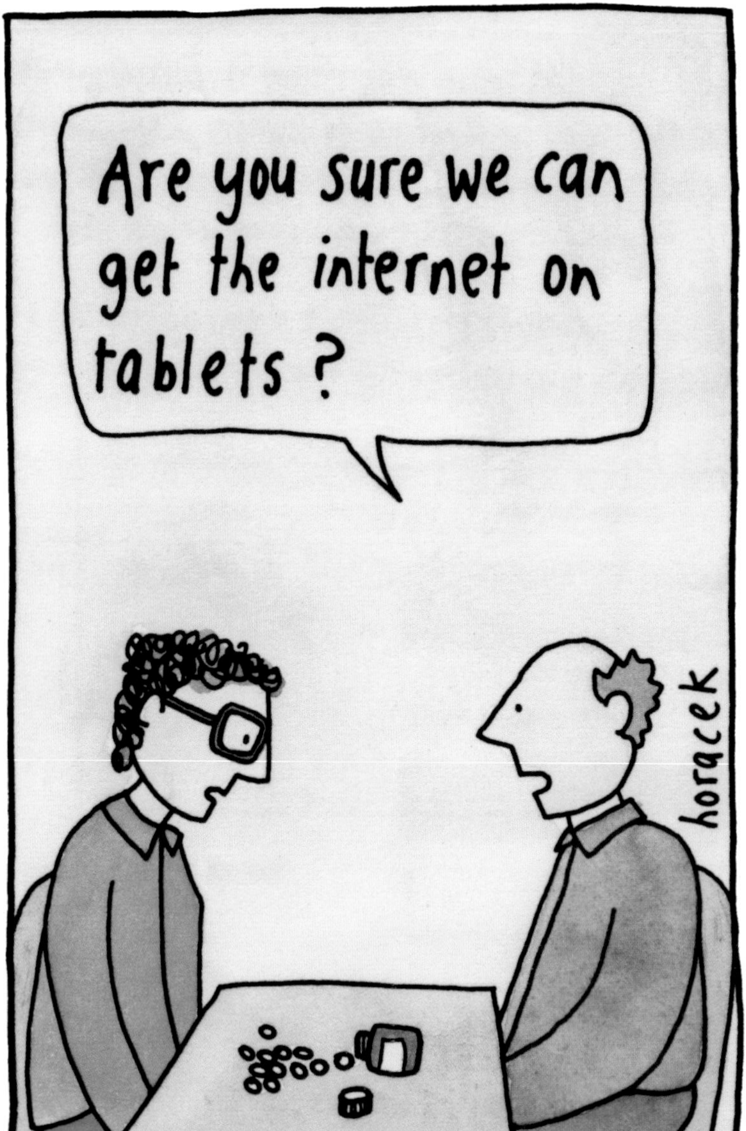
Are you sure we can get the internet on tablets?
horacek

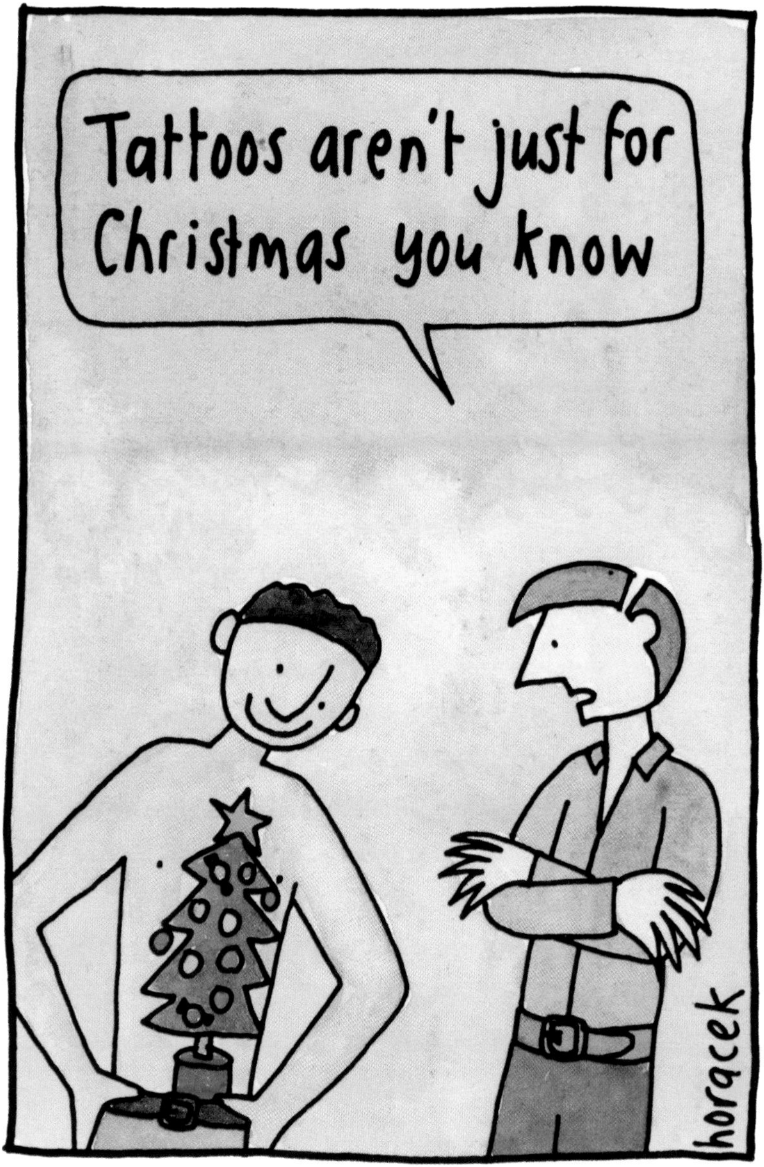
Tattoos aren't just for Christmas you know
horacek

Santa Tortoise
Ho, ho, ho!
I've been waiting for you since 1973
horacek

This snail is set to the Highest Priority
Out of my way!
horacek

ANIMAL COFFEES

cattucino

monkeyato

caffé giraffé

horacek

BEWARE OF THE BATH

There's nothing to F except FOMO itself
I don't think that's quite how the saying goes
horacek

Look here, it isn't all great. Sometimes the various flavours don't resolve themselves into a harmony, the hero of the dish isn't always given the chance to soar, not to mention the possibility of careless plating up which can severely impact on one's enjoyment of the whole meal...
horacek

Baby Talk the Hardline Way
Coochie-coochie-coo, it's off to Nauru with you!
We can stop the boats and stop the childhoods!
horacek

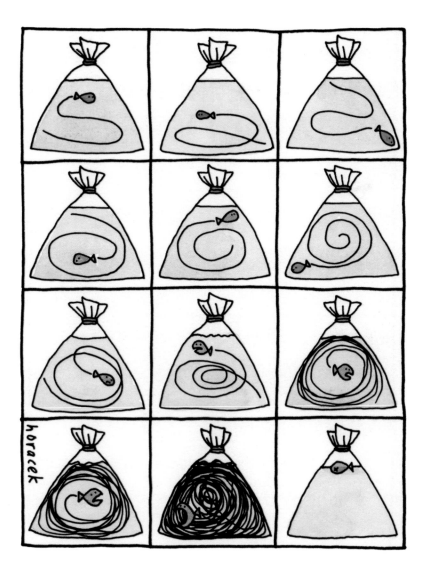

horacek

Autocorrect functions rarely have your best interests at haemorrhoids
Damn...
tap
tap
tap
horacek

Seemed like a good idea at the time No. 67 "Couch Space Ships"
I can't believe we didn't bring the telly...

Beach scenes you will never see : Polite Seagulls
Please, I insist that you take the chip
No, no, absolutely you must have it
horacek

242

243

ACKNOWLEDGEMENTS

My thanks and gratitude to the publications and organisations mentioned in the Introduction, for helping me get my cartoons out into the world in the first instance. Cartoons sitting in a desk drawer are no good to anyone.

Counting my cartoon books and my picture books, this is my seventeenth book, but it is the first one I've ever self-published and it would not have been possible without the commitment to the project of both Fiona Edge and Russ Radcliffe. It is not too much of an exaggeration to say that without their respective interventions at various crucial points, each according to her/his individual expertise, this book would have fallen into a heap any number of times.

Specifically, thanks to Russ for his print-wrangling, for always being available to give answers to my umpteen queries about the finer points of publishing, and particularly for his emergency visit to my studio to help me actually finally begin to put the cartoons in order. And specifically, thanks to Fiona for also always being available, for her wonderful design work and for keeping everything on track in the final stages.

Thanks very much to the inimitable John Clarke for agreeing to write the foreword and doing it so charmingly, and for all the great conversations that have flowed from that about the kind of work we do, and everything else.

Quentin Bryce called me a treasure in a thank you card after I sent her a copy of my picture book *Yellow is My Colour Star*, in honour of the momentous occasion when, wearing a yellow suit, she swore in Julia Gillard as the 27th Prime Minister of Australia. I am grateful that she was also prepared to say this in print on the cover of *Random Life*, and upgrade it to 'absolute treasure' to boot.

Thanks to Jo Bramble, who was extremely generous with her time and publishing knowledge, and who provided much encouragement and excellent advice at many points.

The first step in the creation of this book was the 'Judy Horacek's New Cartoon Book' crowdfunding campaign that I ran through Pozible. Thanks very much to the team there.

Crowdfunding wouldn't achieve anything without people – thanks to all the people who became part of my crowd. My gratitude to everyone who got behind the campaign with such enthusiasm, sending it out far and wide through their networks and/or sending me wonderful messages about

my work. I won't try to name individuals because I don't think I
even saw the half of it. And of course thanks to all the financial
supporters of the campaign, particularly Caroline Sheehan,
Francesca Rendle-Short, Helen Ennis, Helen Maxwell,
Helen Stuckey, Jan and Ivan Horacek, John Horacek, Kate Evans,
Liz O'Brien, Liz Telford, Peter Horacek, the Rimmer-Hamilton
family, Robyn Fortescue, Roz Daniell and Spider Redgold.

Thanks also to Pat Mackle of Avant Card for her constant support
of my work, and for the donation of a free postcard to publicise
my campaign.

Thanks to my manuscript assessors: Chris Cogger, Geraldine Fela,
Bruce Francis, Vig Geddes, Clare Henderson, Kerrie Loveless,
Hannah McCann, Dave McDonald, Jaffa McKenzie,
Ben McKenna, Kylie Nanfro, Brian Newman, Fiona Norris,
Larry O'Loughlin, Alex Oppes, Francesca Rendle-Short, Kate Ross,
Melissa Ross, Eliza Short and Helen Stuckey. Thanks also to
Megan Watson for her final inspection of the cartoons.

Thanks to Kate Ross for admin support, her setting up skills and
her diligent checking and listmaking.

Thank you to Anna Lensky of Pitch Projects and Caitlin Yates of Black Inc Books, who took on *Random Life* to publicise and distribute respectively. Their help has been invaluable and having them involved has allowed me to take this project up to another level.

My gratitude as always to my agent Jenny Darling – although she didn't have much to do with this book specifically, without her *nothing* would ever happen.

There could never be enough space to give my partner Francesca Rendle-Short and the rest of my family and my friends the thanks they deserve, so I'll confine myself to saying, you know who you are, and I love you all very much.